MW01120098

Undoing the Ego Tango

The ABCs of
Getting More of What You Want
More Often with Less Hassle

by Amy Carroll

UNDOING THE EGO TANGO
First edition Green Apple Publishing 2010

First Published Switzerland 2010
by Green Apple Publishing

© Copyright Amy Carroll

All rights reserved. No part of this publication may be reproduced, stored in or introduced into a retrieval system, or transmitted, in any form, or by any means (electronic, mechanical, photocopying, recording or otherwise) without the prior written permission of the publisher.

This book is sold subject to the condition that it shall not, by way of trade or otherwise, be lent, resold, hired out, or otherwise circulated without the publisher's prior consent in any form of binding or cover other than that in which it is published and without a similar condition including this condition being imposed on the subsequent purchaser.

ISBN 978-1-4538-4916-3

Printed by Create Space

Cover designed by Allyson Ingerman
Interior designed by Kim Molyneaux. www.kimmolyneaux.com

Predator, Prey or Partner and Invisible Power Game are registered trademarks of SkillsToSuccess. www.skillstosuccess.com

Images:
Little Girl on Phone © Barbara Campbell

Acknowledgements

This was never meant to be a book. Because you are now reading it means there are many people to thank for that...

Thanks to Rebecca Self for her vision and persistence.

For those of you who loaned me your guidance for structuring and your eyes for editing: Pat Kirkland, Mike Carroll, Kevin Carroll, Bob Gignac, Jo Parfitt (a talented and professional editor), Ellen Snortland (a gifted writer, performer and committed activist), Allyson Ingerman for the cover design and to my multi-talented business manager and book designer, Kim Molyneaux, for always finding the perfect picture.

Many influences have contributed to the concepts in this book. My acknowledgements to the world of improvisational theatre, NVC (non violent communication), NLP (neuro linguistic programming), coaching and Landmark Education.

To my many friends and colleagues who have supported, encouraged and listened to the multiple stories in and about this book: Robbie Kahn, Karen Tse, Paula Cervoni, Dympna Coleman, Madelon Evers, Elli Von Planta, Danielle Gossett, Naima Meriah, Beth Mazzola, Monica Zumstein, Marlene Granger, Robb and Judith Correll, Gaby Müller, Ann Ambiaux, Zoran Todorovic, Tamara Mosegaard, Stefan Heinz, Lisa Sennhauser, Marie O'Hara, Lynn Denton, Dorna Revie, Kristin Engvig, Rosemarie Germain, Katrina Burrus, Karen McCuster, Ania Jakubowski, Rusty Livock, Christine Perey and many more.

To my clients and coachees for their trust and courage in testing out these techniques and sharing their own successes.

And finally to my entire family and Ghislain for your love, laughter and unending support.

foreword

by Ellen Snortland

As a writing coach and author, I deal with a lot of writers, their ideas and the final representation of those ideas – books. Some are good but they are not what I would call evergreen. Folks in the news business use the term 'evergreen' to describe articles you can have on hand and run at any time, because they are 'keepers', always fresh and therefore, evergreen.

Amy Carroll's work, and now her book *Undoing the Ego Tango*, are evergreen. Why? Because we never stop relating to new characters in this play called life. New people create new challenges. We are always in some sort of dance of communication with people that we live, work and play with. Amy teaches us to waltz with people instead of tango... unless you choose to tango, which is a legitimate dance after all. But if you 'tango' as a default and can only do the tango even when the music is a cha-cha, samba or even a polka, you might be stepping on a lot of toes and listening to the beat of a tune your family, friends and colleagues can't even hear. You must untangle your feet if your business partner is tap dancing while you are jitterbugging.

You may have noticed that life does not come with an instruction manual. Rather, we depend on life to teach us the lessons we need. But wait! There are some instruction manuals: books like this one that give you templates for re-choreographing your ways of relating.

My particular field of personal safety starts with the absolutely essential and most important tool of self-defense: your voice. I wrote my book, *Beauty Bites Beast*, because I saw how ill-equipped many people are – especially women and girls – when it comes to saying "no" to unwanted behavior, or asserting themselves when another human being is crossing their boundaries. You could say that females are often rewarded for Prey behaviors, while males are rewarded for Predator strategies. While that's a gross generality with all sorts of exceptions, Carroll lays out the real challenge of all human beings regardless of gender: how to be a Partner. There are a variety of twists and turns when it comes to partnership, and men certainly encounter rigid gender-based expectations that work against them as potential Partners. They are expected to be aggressive – or in Carroll's model, predatory – even if they don't naturally behave that way.

Let me give you a specific example about the inspiration *Undoing the Ego Tango* has given me in my own life. Our family just had a medical emergency and two of us cousins had to go help another grown cousin, who is more like a sister. We all grew up being very close. My other cousin (for the sake of privacy, let's call her Kitty) is very assertive – some might say aggressive – and can't understand why the cousin who needed help (let's call her Bunny) wasn't more vocal and assertive about needing it and getting it. Having just read *Undoing the Ego Tango*, I was able to let Kitty know that Bunny is more 'related' to rabbits, and gets nervous around Kitty because Kitty is more related to mountain lions.

We all know that mountain lions consider rabbits a delectable dinner. Bunny would get a glazed look in her eyes and look like she was about to bolt from the room whenever Kitty and I would come around. Bunny at a cellular level is afraid we will eat her!

While we laughed over this analogy, it made sense to Kitty who has since been able to rein in her feline ways enough to offer partnership to Bunny.

There is a Buddhist saying: *When the student is ready, the teacher appears.* The timing on reading *Undoing the Ego Tango* was like that. The Predator/Prey distinction prepared me for an emergency and made a difference for all of us. I'm grateful to Amy Carroll for her wisdom.

Learning about partnership has benefits at all levels: personal, family, social, business and international relations. Who can't use more Partners?! Carroll teaches us, with entertaining and accessible language, how to take what appears to be discordant music or clumsy dance mates and turn them into graceful colleagues in whatever it is that we want to accomplish. This not only gives us a new understanding and mastery of partnership, but a way to establish a new rhythm for the dance.

With ample anecdotes drawn from all sorts of environments, Ms. Carroll's dancing lessons will have you on the dance floor of life in no time. Wonderful! Fewer broken toes, more music and fun. And if you're in business, there's an added bonus: good partnership will also help the bottom line. Let the dancing begin!

Ellen Snortland
www.snortland.com
Altadena, CA

Undoing the Ego Tango

The ABCs of Getting More of What You Want More Often with Less Hassle

by Amy Carroll

How this book came about...

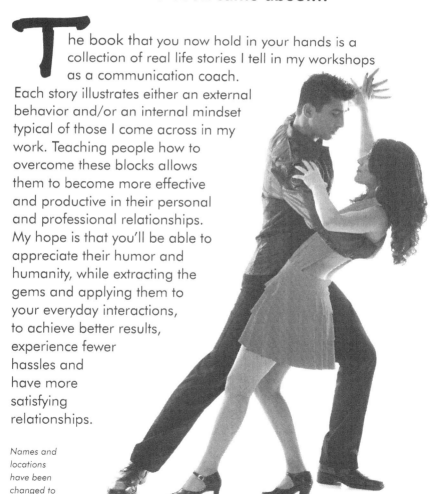

The book that you now hold in your hands is a collection of real life stories I tell in my workshops as a communication coach. Each story illustrates either an external behavior and/or an internal mindset typical of those I come across in my work. Teaching people how to overcome these blocks allows them to become more effective and productive in their personal and professional relationships. My hope is that you'll be able to appreciate their humor and humanity, while extracting the gems and applying them to your everyday interactions, to achieve better results, experience fewer hassles and have more satisfying relationships.

Names and locations have been changed to respect privacy.

A few words about the title

For successful, ongoing, professional and personal relationships, communicating well can sometimes require a bit of fancy footwork. In any kind of human interaction, it's easy to get caught up in what I call the Ego Tango which is triggered by something known as the Invisible Power Game™ (IPG). Most of the time we're unaware that this IPG is going on, causing much of the stress and conflict many of us experience in our communication.

In almost every exchange one person takes the lead, sometimes a negative one, and others follow, whether they intend to or not. When we are not aware of the IPG, we can easily get caught up in the Ego Tango.

The most significant result of my work with clients is simple, and will require practice. This book is a beginner's guide for learning the steps to *Undoing the Ego Tango*. In other words, when your ego has been triggered (you feel disrespected or threatened by someone else), this book will show you how to manage your ego to shift the dynamics, restoring a sense of respect and safety and get more of what you want, more often with less hassle.

So here are the three steps to successfully master this dance:

Create **A**wareness — that your ego has been triggered, leaving you feeling either threatened or disrespected.

Identify **B**ehaviors — that will make you more effective.

Finally **C**hange — the game to experience more collaborative, rewarding relationships.

In each section of *Undoing the Ego Tango* you'll find...

a) a story

b) a Partner Mindset Technique

c) a Moment of Truth: things to think about and ways to put into practice each technique

This book will have a follow up DVD called *Undoing the Ego Tango: Learning the Fancy Footwork* which is currently in the early stages of preparation.

In it, I will demonstrate on camera, the body language as well as other physical tips and tools for getting more of what you want, more often with less hassle.

This book would not have been possible without...

The years of research and development
by Pat Kirkland,
who I'm lucky to have as my sister.

Pat pioneered the communication model:
Predator, Prey or Partner™,
which is the core of the
communication techniques I use
in these stories and in my life.

Opposite are brief definitions of
some of the key terms
from the model.

Glossary

Power: your personal or social power, granted to you by how you show up (how others perceive you). Personal power is separate from positional or hierarchical power, which means anyone can have it, anytime, anywhere!

Predator: is a person who appears over-confident, overly competent or arrogant. A Predator is usually unafraid of conflict and often shows too much respect for themselves and not enough for others.

Prey: is usually a really nice person who will avoid conflict at any cost and who tends to show too much respect for others and not enough for themselves. A person who is a Prey often puts themselves in an inferior position to others, unintentionally inviting mistreatment from others.

Partner: is someone who knows that for communication to be most effective, the power dynamic has to be equal. A Partner does that by showing respect for him or herself and others at the same time.

Invisible Power Game™ (IPG): is an unconscious, non-verbal exchange that happens in the first 30 seconds of an interaction, determining who's got the power, who's in control and most importantly, how you will be treated.

The Predator, Prey or Partner™ model includes both external behaviors (body language, voice and words) and an internal mindset. This book deals primarily with the internal mindset. For more information on Pat, the Predator, Prey or Partner™ model or the Invisible Power Game™, visit www.SkillstoSuccess.com.

This book will give you examples of Predator mishaps, Prey misfortunes as well as Partner-in-action stories and demonstrates ways in which you can shift from Predator or Prey into Partner!

Contents

How I became a
communication coach
and The old Lady
in my Epiphany

How I Became a Communication Coach and The Old Lady in My Epiphany

I call this story my epiphany because it includes the moment when I finally realized I had made a significant improvement in my ability to communicate. To explain this, let's back up a bit...

To the best of my knowledge, I had been picking fights since about the age of six. It was cute for a long time. It only became a problem when, at 15, I started working part-time. My first job was at a fabric store, followed by a florist shop. After a short time, a pattern began to emerge: job after job, I encountered difficult boss after difficult boss. Not being someone to hold my opinion to myself, I would let each of them know in some way, shape or form, exactly how difficult I thought they were. As you can imagine, picking fights with your boss is not likely to earn you the 'employee of the month award'.

The evolving pattern was that having discovered I had yet another difficult boss, I would call my sister, Pat and we'd discuss the situation. She'd listen with great patience and then she'd say, "wow, Amy! You just have really bad luck!"

Fast forward, now a decade into this pattern: eight jobs, eight difficult bosses and eight calls later, it was beginning to dawn on me that nobody has this kind of bad luck! It was glaringly obvious that I was the common denominator. I was doing something to spark the undesirable behavior and conflict in these working situations.

The problem was, I didn't know what I was doing wrong or how to remedy the situation; only that I was perpetuating this predatory pattern.

Deciding to meet the challenge head-on, I read books on the subject, tested out different behaviors, even got therapy (this was long before coaching came along). I was doing a lot to transform my way of interacting with others. In the process, in 1995, I moved to the Swiss Romande region of Switzerland to fulfill my dream of living in a French-speaking country. And, yes, I encountered my share of difficult bosses here as well.

Applying much of what I'd been learning over the past 10 years, I figured I could coach others to shorten their learning curve and reduce the effects of their own communication mishaps. As a result, in 2000, I launched my company, Carroll Communication Coaching. (Yes, my business is focused on helping others improve their communication skills: laugh if you must.)

I was putting every effort into building my contacts and circle of influence when a colleague, Judith, invited me to a networking event in the expatriate community – exactly the target group I wanted to work with more often. That was when I met Francine.

The event kicked off at 6 o'clock with snacks and mingling. Judith said she would arrive at 6:30pm.

"I'll probably get there at 6 o'clock," I told her, ever the keen bean.

Well, the day of the event rolled around and I was busy multitasking. At the last minute, I decided to finish one more project and arrive at 6:30pm, the same time as Judith.

As I walked into the room, Judith's eyes were already boring into my skull. She approached me anxiously.

"Amy, where have you been? I thought you were going to be here at 6 o'clock! I *told* Francine you'd be here at 6 o'clock! She's been waiting for you!"

"Who's Francine?" I innocently asked, having no idea what the problem was. Judith's hands were balled into fists and her stress level was palpable.

"Francine's this 85-year-old woman who's not very comfortable in social situations, so I told her you'd spend the first half hour with her!"

It didn't seem fair to hold Judith responsible, I thought, she had good intentions, and I didn't feel guilty because I couldn't have known of this arrangement.

Judith mumbled, "well… come on in anyway, I'll introduce you to Francine…"

We walked in to a room packed with people and yet it was impossible not to miss seeing a statuesque older woman with a giant beehive hair-do, Francine. There were two other women standing like guards, one on either side of her. I approached Francine to introduce myself and held out my hand. Francine shot me a steely look.

"I have been waiting for you for half an hour! Where have you been?" she barked.

My first thought was, *girlfriend... you are messing with the wrong short person!* (I'm 4 ft 10½ in/150 cm on a very good hair day.)

Let me interrupt this scene to explain to you, dear reader, that I have a lively and entertaining imagination. In my mind, I instantly saw my possible options. Luckily, before I actually opened my mouth, I realized my ego had been triggered, so I reviewed my alternatives. My first imaginary reply was my default to the Predator response, sounding something like this: *sweetheart, if you haven't gotten your act together by the time you're your age, there's nothing I can do for you!* (accompanied by a swagger, head tilt, lots of eye rolling and a sarcastic smile).

Being verbally attacked in a social situation by a complete stranger made this response very tempting and some of you may think, even justified. The thing was, I didn't want to be rude to a woman I didn't even know. Equally motivating, the English-speaking community in Switzerland is rather small and I was fairly new in town. Selfishly, I didn't want to alienate myself by coming across as nasty in front of the other two women. The last thing I wanted to do was damage my reputation before I'd even built it!

Then I thought, what if I take the opposite path, the one of the Prey? In this case I could go all apologetic and meek by whimpering, *Francine, I'm really sorry. I didn't mean to. It will never happen again. Please forgive me* (accompanied by lots of anxious movement, skittish eye contact and a bowing head). In addition to my rich imagination, I have an exceptionally strong ego. I can tell you right now, my ego was never going to let me respond like that.

At this point, I was feeling a bit stuck, until suddenly I remembered something I had learned in improvisational theater: **for communication to be effective, the power dynamic has to be equal. The way to equalize the power dynamic is to show respect for yourself and for the other person simultaneously.** In that moment, I was able to coach myself. *OK, Amy,* I thought, *keep your body still, hold direct eye contact, put a warm smile on your face and* *keep your voice calm*. So I did all those things and then without any sarcasm in my voice (which I'm not sure how I managed), I reached out my hand.

"Francine, if I had known you were waiting for me, it would have been a pleasure to spend the time with you. It's nice to meet you," I said, beaming with upbeat and friendly energy.

At that moment, she shook my hand and smiled, melting like an ice cream cone in Texas in August. It was amazing! After that, she was absolutely lovely to me for the rest of the evening.

This was my moment of realization, my epiphany. I can't tell you how tempting it was to peek up at the skies to see if the clouds had parted and the angels were singing. For the first time, I realized that by being conscious there was an Invisible Power Game™ going on and putting my ego to one side, I could choose different behaviors over my instinctive reaction and get a very different response. That, for me, really was my moment of awakening to the power I have when I'm aware I can choose different behaviors and change the game.

It was such a shock to become aware of myself, to see the dynamics at play and to have the ability to instantly shift the status of my relationship. What a huge amount of freedom for all my future interactions with people! Today I practice using these Partner mindset techniques in a wide variety of situations. As a result, the level of conflict in my life has reduced dramatically and both my professional life and personal life have benefited significantly.

The important thing to take away is that there is so much **power in awareness**. That's the first step. **Start to notice when the Invisible Power Game™ has been set in motion and observe your own reaction to it. Do you become aggressive or defensive towards someone else? Keep in mind, regardless of how anyone else may behave, you always have the choice of how you respond. For now, just begin to pay attention.**

Moment of Truth

So here's your first assignment:

Practice becoming aware. Write down the
last five to ten times you found yourself losing
your composure, became agitated, anxious or
defensive in communication with others.

_____

_____

_____

What thought process went on in your head?
How did you feel? How did you notice your ego
was triggered?

_____

_____

_____

What happened? What words were used?
Be sure to stick with just the facts.

_____

_____

_____

Make Up a
Different Story

When someone is behaving in a way that I perceive as negative or somehow disrespectful, I practice the technique of making up a different story. I believe the idea came from a book called *The Dark Side of the Light Chasers*, by Debbie Ford, where she talks about making up a different interpretation.

The idea of applying the 'Make up a Different Story' technique first came to me several years ago while driving on the highway from Zurich to Bern. It was early evening when a car came flying past me in the left lane. The man was driving so fast and so dangerously that I almost had an accident.

Well, you can imagine some of the choice comments I made about him for the next 20 minutes. After I calmed down a bit, I started thinking about an explanation as to why he might be driving like that. What could possibly have motivated his behavior? I started coming up with 'reasons': perhaps he was late for an appointment, forgot something back at the office, didn't want to miss the start of his favorite team's final football match? None of the 'reasons' seemed good enough, until I thought of this one... his wife must have been having a baby! Yup, that was the excuse that worked for me. That was a good enough reason to explain the reckless driving.

I noticed, after coming up with this explanation that I immediately calmed down and had empathy for the guy. This is the whole point of the technique, to move yourself from feeling angry or defensive towards another person to having empathy and a bit of understanding for them. It probably helped that I once knew a guy whose wife actually did deliver their baby in the car, and yet it doesn't matter whether the actual explanation is true or not. Making up another story will help calm you down, which is the most important benefit and encourage you to stay in Partner mode while interacting with the other person.

Another example of this powerful technique comes from Stephen Covey's book *The 7 Habits of Highly Effective People*. Covey tells of a time he was travelling in a subway when a man gets in with his two sons, the sons are running all over the place bothering the people. As this continues, Covey gets more and more annoyed until finally he gets irritated enough to ask the father why he doesn't do something to control his kids. The father replies, "we just got back from the hospital where their mother died. I don't know how to handle it and I guess they don't either."

For me, this is a profound example that I can't always know the truth or know why people do the things they do and I may never know 'the truth'. The problem is that often the assumptions I construct cause me to feel more annoyed or defensive towards the other person. I discovered the best thing I can do for myself is make up a different story to shift my internal attitude, allowing me to offer them empathy and understanding while keeping me in Partner mode. The bonus is that this increases the chances of getting a more positive outcome.

TESTIMONIAL

... from Tom, a finance manager with a multinational software company: "Last month my colleague sent an email to the entire team stating I had neglected to acknowledge the hard work of two other team members during an end-of-the-quarter presentation. At first I felt angry and defensive, telling myself, he's trying to make me look bad. After a few minutes of ranting, I realized I actually had no clue if that was his intention so I thought about another story I could 'make up'. With a bit of brain/storming (and a good workout at the gym), I told myself, 'he feels frustrated and jealous about my recent promotion'. This helped me to relax. Later when I talked to him about the email, I was much calmer and we sorted it out in five minutes."

Bureaucrats in Action:
Another one Bites the Dust

Bureaucrats in Action:
Another One Bites the Dust

t was June of 2005. On a balmy Sunday after hiking in the French Alps, I arrived back at my car to discover the window broken and my purse stolen. (OK, OK... I know I should have hidden it better.) Now, if this has happened to you, you know the whole thing can be upsetting– the damage to the car, the hassle of calling all your credit card companies, let alone losing your favorite lipstick. It can be stressful, to say the least. What I was really worried about, though, was my passport. This posed a significant concern because I was scheduled to travel to London in just ten days for the start of a huge project with a new client.

Monday morning, I called the US Embassy. I was in problem-solving mode and asked the man who answered the phone what I needed to do to make my business trip possible.

"No problem. We can issue you with a temporary passport," he said. I was so relieved, I can't tell you.

"Fabulous," I said. "May I come in on Thursday to collect it?"

"Fine! We'll see you then," he said and hung up the phone.

Thursday rolled around and I got up early. I arrived at 8:30am and was the second person in line; I was most impressed with myself. I waited my turn, then approached the window, thinking this was just a matter of paperwork.

I hadn't even finished explaining my situation when the woman behind the bullet-proof glass, let's call her Beverley, began scolding me.

"Somebody could have been using your passport for four days and you're just reporting it now?!" she exclaimed. "Why didn't you come in sooner?" She looked down at the passport-sized photographs I'd brought. "And those aren't even the right size, you'll have to get new ones."

REJECTED

I was shocked by her response. As calmly as possible, I explained that I'd spoken to a gentleman at the Embassy who told me I could get a temporary passport in time for my business trip the following week to London.

"There aren't any men working here," she said abruptly at the very moment that a man walked behind her desk. It took great restrain not to call this gentleman to her attention.

There's one thing I'd like you to keep in mind here, because I sure was: I was still getting my own business up and running. This trip to London was for a major new multinational client. Missing this trip, for this client, was not an option. It was essential that I receive my temporary passport and time was running out.

The next thing I knew, Beverley squared her shoulders and looking smug, said, "…and besides, this isn't urgent, you live here, you don't need to get back to the States. The Consul won't approve this." She raised her eyes as if to dismiss me and call the next person in line forward.

It was at that moment that I felt my life flash before my eyes (or maybe it was Beverley's life). I realized I needed to use every communication skill I had ever learned or taught anyone in order to manage myself and get what I needed.

So instead of reacting like a Prey, whining, crying and begging (which might have gotten me what I wanted yet would have been rather humiliating) or acting like a Predator, saying *now I know why they make that glass bullet proof!* (which definitely would NOT have gotten me what I wanted), I took a deep breath and moving and speaking slowly, without a hint of sarcasm in my voice, I said, "do you think you could ask the Consul?"

"No," she snapped.

I was running out of options. Whatever I did next it was imperative that I stayed in Partner.

"Do you think you could just check with the Consul?"

She gave me another hostile, "NO!" and did the eye-raising thing again.

With the second rejection, I sat down to fill out the papers she had given me, only to discover that, due to the anger-induced adrenaline pulsing through me, I could barely read the writing on the form. I looked up and noticed a couple sitting across from me with a look of empathic disbelief on their faces. We exchanged a series of non-verbals which essentially translated to, *major bummer, what a hassle. Sure hope you have better luck.* This brief moment of bonding and connecting with the couple helped me to lighten up a bit, shake off some of my frustration and refocused me to drag myself back into Partner. After about five minutes I had completed the paperwork and had calmed down enough to refocus on what was essential: walking out with my temporary passport.

Now I was ready to return the paperwork to Beverley, who was nowhere to be found. I waited. About 15 minutes later when Beverley still had not come back to the window, I decided to go to the second window. You can imagine my surprise when I found the phantom male right there! I approached him hesitantly, sliding the paperwork under the partition. He asked me a few questions, all of which were easy enough to answer, though I still had a strong sense of foreboding.

"Go to the cashier's window and pay for your temporary passport," he said.

I was shocked and ecstatic! Seizing the opportunity before it vanished, I moved quickly, hoping Beverley would not appear to intercede in my great fortune... only to discover her at the cashier's window!

Beverley squared her shoulders again.

"What did you tell the Consul?" she asked through bared teeth.

I calmly explained that I answered his questions and he told me to come over here and pay.

"Well, I talked to him and we decided to make an exception." Unbelievable, now she wants to take the credit, amazing!

With all the good will and playfulness I could muster I said, "oh, Beverley, thank you so much! I could hug you!" We laughed together and she took my money.

I didn't know I had truly won Beverley over until this happened:

"Oh, and by the way, we can use those photos you have with you today for the temporary passport. Here's an envelope with a stamp already on it, addressed to me. You can just mail the photos when you get them taken... oh, and here's a map of where to find the right type of photo machine at the train station," she said with a wide smile.

Amazed and surprised by this dramatic shift in Beverley's behavior, I decided to see just how far I could go. "Beverley," I said tentatively, "could you tell me how to get to the Paraguayan Embassy?" She responded enthusiastically, "sure, let me get the address for you." A minute later she returned with the address and a map highlighting which tram I could take to get there! In front of my eyes,

Beverley had transformed from Nasty Predator to Playful Partner.

Two weeks later, when I mailed my photos to her, I put in a short, friendly, handwritten thank you note.

A month later when I realized the Paraguayan Embassy would not issue a visa in a temporary passport, what did I do? Called my buddy, Beverley! In a friendly, upbeat manner, I explained the situation and asked if I could fax her my residence permit to get my permanent passport processed immediately.

"Sorry, I can only accept faxes from official offices," Beverley explained. "You'll have to go to the Consulate near you. Here's the phone number, talk to my colleague, Jonas and he will help you," came her enthusiastic reply.

I made a couple of phone calls and realized there was no way I'd be able to get to the Consulate in time that day. So I called my new best friend, Beverley back! Hard to believe, isn't it? I explained that it would take me almost two hours to get there and then I paused. The pausing is important. Practice pausing. Create a little room for partnership and step back to see if people will step into that position.

"Hmmmm, two hours..." Beverley hesitated. "Well, why don't you fax it to me then?" The official rule she couldn't change earlier had become much more flexible indeed!

Over the years, Beverley has turned into a fantastic Partner and resource – she even helps my friends. When one colleague used her services recently, Beverley said, "hey, if Amy's ever leading a workshop nearby, she should tell me! I'd love to attend."

Make Your
Partner Look Good

This concept comes from improvisational theater and is referred to as 'having an improv attitude'. It's an essential part of the Partner mindset. This is particularly important when there is potential for conflict and you don't know how to respond. Or more accurately, the response you are considering is not going to improve the situation and may even make things worse.

In these moments, ask yourself, *how can I make my Partner look good? Right now in this situation?* (Your Partner is anyone you are interacting with at the moment, for example, a colleague, airline check-in person, police officer, Beverley and so on.) Just asking yourself the question will start to change your mindset and the response that follows, for example, you could: ask them a question, offer a genuine compliment, ask for help or offer a warm smile. In Beverley's case, letting her take credit for getting the job done allowed her to shift into Partner with me. Whatever works! One example I use often is when I come across a grumpy customer service person at the grocery store, post office or by phone, working at a call center. If it's towards the end of the day, I might ask, "is it the end of your shift soon?" If they say, "yes," I might reply with a, "well I wish you a well-deserved, relaxing evening". If they say, "no, I've got four more hours," I might say, "well I hope the rest of your shift is not

too stressful." More often than not, their energy picks up and they are just a little more friendly.

Here is an example of a time when I failed miserably by not applying my own advice.

Several years ago, I remember going to the Geneva airport, heading for Paris. When flying to France from Geneva, it's necessary to go through the French passport control. On this particular day, accustomed to passport control being in another location, I strolled by the desk, not noticing the guard sitting there. In response to my apparent show of disrespect, the guard responded by banging her hand on the desk with great force several times, then asking in a very sarcastic, hostile manner, " do you need glasses?" Needless to say, I got seriously triggered by her attitude and in my very best French and most sarcastic tone, I shot back a retort. Suffice to say, we exchanged several rounds of insults, descending to the point of the guard insulting my French (which is not particularly difficult to do). It was about this time that I realized, if I continued, I might be invited to spend some time in a small room for an extended period.

The good news was that I did manage to get to Paris on the intended flight, the bad news was my enormous disappointment in my behavior towards this guard. Even though many might agree with me that 'she had it coming', it's not a shining example of the Partner attitude to which I aspire. I reflected on this incident for several days. I must admit, it took a while to pull myself out of my feelings of indignation.

Eventually I was able to start asking myself, *how could I have made my Partner look good?* I began imagining Partner-like responses to the same scenario. Then I remembered that just after she had sarcastically asked the question, "do you need glasses?" I had been walking back to the desk and noticed she was wearing the coolest, most extraordinary glasses. My newly created 'make your Partner look good' response could have been, *well, no and if I did, I would be delighted to have glasses like yours. Those are amazing!* (delivered with a warm smile and enthusiasm).

Can you imagine the likely effect this would have had on the woman? She may have been momentarily perplexed and probably would not have been able to maintain the same level of aggressiveness towards me. Just noticing a minor shift in her behavior would have felt like an achievement.

More often than not, when I am able to successfully 'make my Partner look good' (even if internally I am feeling less then friendly) it feels like a victory, because it shows me I am able to override my instinctual reaction and choose a response that will lead to better interactions and desired results.

My recommendation: reflect on past interactions which you may be less than proud of and flex the Partner mindset muscle by brainstorming alternative responses (enlisting friends may be helpful here). Even though the incident is past, getting your brain to imagine new ways of responding will create a new pathway in your brain and increase your chances of success in the future.

TESTIMONIAL

...from Phillip, product manager with a multinational household products company: "I have a colleague who I have never gotten along with. Recently, I started pretending we were buddies and when he comes by my desk, instead of saying what I used to say which was, 'what do you want?' (in a semi-annoyed tone), I've started saying (with an upbeat tone) 'how can I help you, Jeff?' It's incredible how much it has changed the way we interact. In fact, I kind of like the guy now, amazing."

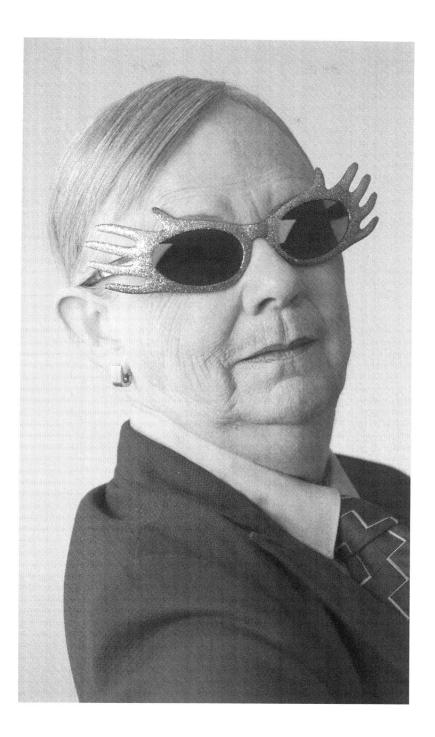

Moment of Truth

Name some people in your life with whom staying in Partner is sometimes difficult for you (neighbors, colleagues, relatives):

....

....

....

What are some specific scenarios where you defaulted with a Predator or Prey response:

....

....

....

Now imagine alternative 'Partner' responses to the same situations that would make your Partner look good:

....

....

....

Stay Calm

Particularly in a moment of tension or conflict, I cannot over-emphasize the importance of appearing calm. What matters is that you give this perception when you are interacting with others. This means moving slowly, speaking slowly, allowing a back and forth flow in the conversation and resisting the temptation to force your point of view. Behaving in this way will most likely diminish the conflict and reduce it to a simple dialogue. Internally, you may not actually feel calm; that's OK. The positive effect will be reflected in the other person, who will begin to calm down and be more willing to listen to your perspective. Your chances of being heard will be increased and therefore, the chances of you getting more of what you want will increase!

TESTIMONIAL

... from Andreas, head of procurement with a multinational pharmaceutical company. "Last month I was at a customer briefing center when this guy comes up to me and started yelling at me about some issue that had nothing to do with me. Instead of trying to calm him down or talk over him in order to explain myself, I simply stood still, kept eye contact and let him know I was listening (actually I was more interested in getting my heart rate to slow down enough to avoid passing out). What was surprising to me was how quickly he calmed down and excused himself."

Moment of Truth

First think of a situation where you 'lost your cool'. Now note some of your personal cues or non-verbal signals that may have indicated to yourself or others you were losing your composure (for example, your heart began to race, you were breathing faster, speaking faster, louder, interrupting the other person, using a sarcastic or condescending tone, you had raised eye brows and so on). If you are not sure, ask someone who has seen you lose your composure. Be sure to ask someone who is not afraid to speak openly to you.

_____

_____

_____

What other behaviors can you replace them with the next time you begin to notice these signals (for example, slow, deep breaths, relaxed face, warm smile, nodding your head, other non-verbal acknowledgements that you are listening, relaxed eye brows and so on)?

_____

_____

_____

TO DO LIST-

- breathe

- smile

- listen

The Whiner
and the Wine

The Whiner and the Wine

It was a beautiful, warm September day, a Sunday and I was headed to a wine tour in Montreux. Now, if there's one thing you learn quickly as a newcomer to Switzerland, it is that the Swiss are always on time! Everything is punctual. This was a walking wine tour that would depart from a tiny wine cellar at precisely twelve noon, snake along the hillside vineyards, eventually reaching a spectacular view and awaiting lunch. If I was not there on time I would miss the tour, lose my 50 francs and worse still, not have the opportunity to enjoy this wonderful, sunny day out wandering among the hillside vines.

I was running late and already a bit stressed when I hit the post-church traffic. In fact, I was just getting off the highway when I should have been strolling towards the wine cellar. I took the lane I thought would get me to the starting point as quickly as possible. It turned out that the road was blocked and I was in the wrong lane!

I needed to be in the left lane so that I could turn, park my car and run to the cellar just in time for the tour to begin.

The problem was that in the left lane there was a big, white delivery truck. The driver of the truck was a bulky man with a bushy moustache and cigarette hanging from his mouth. I had the impression he wasn't too excited about working on this beautiful Sunday.

To complicate matters, he had a red light and my lane had a green light. I had to find a solution – fast. It occurred to me that I could indicate to the truck driver that I needed to turn in front of him. Since his windows were up, I gave him a warm smile, friendly look and non-verbally mimed to him, *could I turn in front of you?*

Well, apparently I had been spot on about him not having a good day and this request must have pushed him over the edge. His mimed response was filled with wildly aggressive and offensive gestures. Angry arms flying, fingers pointing skywards, the equivalent of words I'm sure I don't even know in French!

My fantasy response was to channel the former New York driver in me and show him a thing or two! As extremely satisfying as this would have been, it would have certainly meant missing my wine tour. Being conscious that the Invisible Power Game™ was at play, I made a quick

decision. Pretending not to notice his behavior, I responded with a bigger smile and mimed, *oh, great! So it's OK to go in front of you?* Of course, privately I felt a little stupid.

Here was the payoff....

At first he looked exasperated and frustrated then surprised and confused. He just shrugged his shoulders and indicated, *OK, lady... go ahead of me.*

I felt such a rush of satisfaction at being able to maintain my composure and not react to his aggressive behavior... and I got exactly what I wanted! I practically skipped through the entire wine tour.

The lesson to take from this:

Pretend Not to Notice

Fight the urge or 'pretend not to notice'. That is, when the other person is being an idiot, jerk, loser, whatever you want to call it, resist the temptation to react or point this out to them. Pretending not to notice when the other person is being difficult and instead continuing to behave like a strong Partner, will have a duel benefit. First of all, if you don't engage the other person, it makes it difficult for them to continue acting that way because it's pretty tough for people to fight alone. After a certain point, they realize they are going to look stupid if they continue misbehaving. The second benefit of this technique, by not acknowledging their difficult behavior, you help them to 'save face', which makes it that much easier for them to step into your frame (see Technique 4) and start behaving more respectfully towards you!

Disclaimer: I'm not suggesting you allow yourself to be mistreated by others. By all means, if after using this technique three to five times, their behavior continues or resurfaces in the future, I strongly recommend addressing this with them and ideally when tempers are calm. If you are unsure how to do this, I suggest using a simple method developed by Marshall Rosenberg called NVC (non-violent communication) in his book, *Nonviolent Communication: A Language of Life*. Although the name may sound intimidating, I have used and taught this straightforward method to others for several years with great success.

For me, pretending not to notice is like the martial art of Aikido. Some call it **Emotional Aikido**. When I can successfully suppress my ego and get a positive outcome, I'm practicing the Partner mindset.

Along with the Italian philosopher, Daniel Verde, my brother, Kevin, says it beautifully: "Positive Influence is the art of helping others get your way."

Partner Mindset Technique No.3

TESTIMONIAL

... from Francis, technical director with a telecommunications company: "During a conference call last week with a client, I really had to pretend not to notice when this client started complaining about our team's incompetence and lack of follow through. He was upset because an important installation was delayed and he was blaming us. Well, it turned out that his assistant never placed the order because he hadn't approved the budget. It was so hard not to make some sarcastic comment. Instead, I said, 'hey, no problem, we have the order now, let's see what we can do to get this installed asap.' By the way, he sent me an email the next day apologizing for his comments and thanking me for my follow through!"

Partner Mindset
Reading Suggestion

Thinking of **Emotional Aikido**, I am reminded of a book written by Professor George Kohlrieser, internationally recognized expert on leadership. In his book, *Hostage at the Table: How Leaders Can Overcome Conflict, Influence Others and Raise Performance* (http://www.hostageatthetable.com), Professor Kohlrieser, who is a leadership professor as well as a hostage negotiator, takes the physical reality of actually being a hostage to the metaphorical level. He shows how living as a 'psychological hostage' is like living with a gun to your head. You are not in the same literal danger as a real hostage, yet you are powerless to act. Any one of us can be 'held hostage' by people, by situations and, not least, by our own emotions. Think back to my earlier example with the French customs officer. That was a classic case of hijacking and I wasn't even on the plane!

Moment of Truth

With whom in your life do you get triggered regularly (such as colleagues, family, customer service workers)?

_____

_____

_____

When was the last time you could have pretended not to notice and didn't? What got in your way? What stopped you (for example, wanting to prove you were right, to show the other person they were wrong, wanting to let off steam)?

_____

_____

_____

What can you do, specifically, in those moments, to pretend not to notice (such as smile, continue asking questions, keeping upbeat energy, friendly tone)?

_____

_____

_____

You may be concerned that pretending not to notice will make you look incompetent or be mistreated. How is pretending not to notice actually powerful for both parties involved? What are the benefits to you?

_____

_____

_____

With whom might you practice this over the next few days? It could be with someone close to you or a stranger. In the moment, what can you do, specifically?

_____

_____

_____

Notice how this shifts the focus from what they're doing to how you're responding. When you start to have the ability to manage your own ego, you have begun to master these techniques. The results will be surprising!

The key to
Household Harmony

The Key to Household Harmony

Also known as 'The Mom and Dad Story'

To preface this story, I must say, I have two of the most amazing, supportive parents a kid could want. With that in mind, I hope they won't disown me for taking artistic license with the following story.

My parents, Bud and Claire, have been happily married for over 56 years. Like all couples, they have great moments as well as occasional 'not so pretty' moments. For the readers' benefit, here is an example of a not so pretty scenario between my parents.

Imagine my dad, Bud, is in the kitchen, Mom's in the living room.

"Claire, where are the car keys?!" says Bud, in an annoyed, slightly condescending tone. Mom hears the words. She also hears the tone and the unspoken *idiot* at the end of the sentence.

Getting immediately triggered, Claire matches his semi-muffled, antagonistic tone.

"I don't know Bud, you had them last!!"

Now Claire's pleased because she got to turn it back on him. In fact, she has one-upped Bud with concrete evidence of his apparent lack of intelligence. The problem is, the evening they will have as a result of this exchange is not likely to be a 'Norman Rockwell' moment.

The good news is that three of their seven kids are full-time communication coaches. Imagine the same interaction after one of them, in this case, my mom, has gotten a little free coaching. Let's rewind the scene with that in mind: Bud is in the kitchen.

"Claire, where are the car keys?!" he says, using the same tone as before.

Mom hears the message, and just before she instinctively reacts, she remembers something one of her very clever children has told her. She pauses, takes a deep breath and chooses to respond in a calm, confident, gentle tone.

"I don't know, Bud, let me come help you find them."

Something you should know about my dad, he's a smart man. Bud knows that if he keeps using such a nasty tone, he's going to start looking stupid. Instead, he responds in a more positive, respectful way with something like, "no problem, thanks. I'll keep looking." Because my mother chose a different response, my father's behavior has been positively shifted.

The Frame Game

As we communicate with each other, human beings construct different frames. Frames are like the mood, tone, environment or ambience of an interaction. Frames can be positive (friendly, playful, respectful, energizing, for example) or negative (tense, angry, disrespectful, bored, perhaps). We set frames through our body language, voice and the words we use.

Unconsciously, we are constantly setting frames and being invited into others' frames. The danger is, that when we're not aware of another person's frame, we can get caught in it like a trap. Positive frames are not usually a concern. It's when we get caught in others' negative frames that can cause problems.

In the first interaction, Dad set up a 'blame game' frame and because Mom wasn't aware, she fell into it. Because she was unconscious about the negative frame, she reacted defensively, resulting in negative consequences for them both. In the second interaction, Dad set up the same frame. This time, because Mom was conscious of it and aware she had a choice, she thought, *hmm… I don't think I like that frame. I think I'm going to create another one.* So she constructed a more positive and inviting frame, which was naturally appealing to my father. She could not force him in. She made the frame so appealing (holding respect for both herself and my father) that he chose to step in, resulting in a more enjoyable evening for both of them and their visiting children.

Partner Mindset Technique No. 4

What is important to remember is that you have a choice whether or not to step into another person's frame. First you must be conscious of what the frame is (awareness). Second you may need to put your ego to the side and use different behaviors. Third, change the frame to a more positive game and watch the results!

Partner Mindset Technique No. 4

Moment of Truth

Whose frames, both positive and negative, do you fall into (colleague, partner, neighbor, check-out clerk, for example)?

_____

_____

_____

What kinds of frames, both positive and negative, do you set up in your personal or professional life?

_____

_____

_____

What can you do to set up more powerful partnership frames? What might you have to pretend not to notice?

_____

_____

_____

booze, blues
and all that jazz

Booze, Blues
and all that Jazz

I t was July 2005, at a booth along Lac Leman during the International Montreux Jazz Festival. Every year, this giant seasonal event rolls out, with hundreds of artisans displaying their jewelry and pottery, scarves and other wares accompanied by music for just about every preference. It was about 1 o'clock in the morning on a Saturday night. A friend and I were admiring a beautiful display of jewelry; the artist had set out all his rings in neat rows according to size – small, medium and large, all the way down a long table.

Just then, a rather tall, middle-aged guy came staggering over to the display. Obviously extremely drunk, he stumbled towards the table and grabbed a handful of rings.

"How much for these?!" he slurred, steadying himself against the table with his other hand, still holding a half-full wine bottle.

The beautiful arrangement was ruined. The artist didn't seem to know how to handle it, so he tried to ignore the man. My internal reaction to this man's behavior was fierce and immediate. I wanted to toss the big idiot to the ground, lecture him on his disrespectful behavior and obvious over indulgence then insist he apologize to the artist. Being coherent enough to realize this was a fantasy likely to end badly, I grudgingly moved to the other end of the table, as far away from him as possible attempting to distract myself, mostly because I didn't trust myself to resist giving in to a Predator reaction. Well, I had done such a good job avoiding him that the next thing I knew, I was standing next to his girlfriend! Out of nowhere, with no preparation, no conscious thought, I turned to her and put on my low, gentle, voice. "Do you think you could ask him to stop doing that? It's kind-of disrespectful to the man," I said in my very best French while pointing to the artist.

She whipped around in a not surprisingly drunken fashion to face her beau.

"Honey, this woman wants to say something to you!" she slurred.

Oh, great, I thought. The next thing I knew, I was face-to-face (OK, face-to-chest is more accurate) with the drunk guy. Without missing a beat, I said the same thing to him in the same low, gentle voice.

"Do you think you could stop doing that? It's kind-of disrespectful to the man."

"I just wanna get my ear pierced," he bellowed back, wavering slightly on his feet.

What I wanted to say was, *what the hell does that have to do with anything*?! Instead, resisting the distraction to be pulled off topic, I said the same thing in the same calm, respectful tone of voice (as if he'd never brought up the subject of ear piercing).

"Do you think you could stop doing that? It's kind-of disrespectful to the man."

A few moments later, without commotion or comment, he and his girlfriend turned and slowly staggered away.

So often, situations like this one escalate out of control or at least become aggressive and disrespectful. What worked this time? What can we learn from this story? Reflecting upon this experience, two things became apparent to me:

First, by speaking to him calmly, making eye contact and using a gentle tone of voice, I sent a message of respect for him. In my words and attitude, I implied that if he'd known he was being disrespectful to the artist, then of course he would not have behaved like that. It was a way of helping him to 'save face'. (Of course, I had to pretend not to notice and resist the temptation to point out to him what an idiot I thought he was being. As satisfying as this may have been, it wasn't going to get me the result I wanted.) What was so amazing was that the message penetrated his drunken state. I discovered these skills work with people who are out of control – and can diffuse a wide variety of tense or difficult situations at home and work!

The second discovery I made was that, despite my anger towards his behavior, I was able to choose a respectful response that got me what I wanted. My newly developed instinct successfully overrode my ego! My belief is that because I've been practicing these communication techniques frequently in various settings (personal and professional), they have become my new way of being... most of the time. It's like the analogy of learning a martial art. When you master the art, you develop a new reflex. This story emphasizes the importance of going to the gym, working out, so to speak, practicing these techniques and behaviors in short encounters, on a regular basis so that they become integrated, instinctual and part of your new way of being. It's like upgrading your hard drive (aka your brain).

When you are able to use these behaviors automatically in stressful situations, you'll know your practice has paid off!

The Broken Record Approach

Partner Mindset Technique No.5

An explanation to readers who may not be familiar with vinyl records. Back in the days before iPods, before CDs, before cassette tapes and 8 tracks, we had records. Being rather delicate items, they could be easily scratched, which meant the recording often got 'stuck', repeating the same sound over and over. Thus the term 'broken record' was born.

While this technique is simple and straightforward, it also needs awareness to be able to apply it. Often when others are upset or angry, perhaps feeling guilty or responsible, they will attempt to pull the conversation off course with multiple distractions. (Magicians refer to it as creating 'smoke and mirrors' to divert the audience's attention.) The person you are interacting with might come up with unrelated excuses or attempt to turn the responsibility to yourself or someone else. You need to be aware this may happen. Avoid getting pulled off course by resisting the temptation to discuss other issues, or defend yourself (internally your ego may be triggered). Instead keep repeating your request or question, using the same calm tone of voice consistently. Eventually, the other person will understand they can not wiggle their way out of the situation. The result is usually compliance or agreement.

The calm tone is extremely important to maintain. Otherwise, if you allow frustration or sarcasm to leak out through your tone, it will indicate to the other person they got you. Plus, maintaining the calm tone is signaling respect to the other which makes them more willing to comply more quickly. (I'm told this approach is also successful with unreasonable requests from kids and adolescents.)

Partner Mindset Technique No. 5

TESTIMONIAL

... from Chris, HR director with a multinational software company: "I had a VP come up to me during our quarterly budgeting meeting and tell me there was no way he could comply with the reduction in head count. He had a dozen reasons why HR shouldn't be involved in the head count discussions. Instead of getting into a debate with him on all his different reasons (which I would have done in the past), I resisted the temptation to justify and just repeated myself, 'Gary, I can imagine this puts you in a tough position and this is what needs to happen.' I must have said it three times and by the fourth time, Gary seemed to lose his steam and said, 'ya I know, this is what needs to happen.'"

Moment of Truth

When, in your life, do you find yourself in a conversation where you agree to something you hadn't intended? Or you feel confused or manipulated by the outcome?

_____

_____

_____

What might be an appropriate 'broken record' response you could have used?

_____

_____

_____

What are the payoffs to you when you use the 'broken record' response?

_____

_____

_____

Where is your practice gym? Where are your opportunities to practice at home, work and everywhere in between (for example, after a tough day at work, how can you step into Partner with a sales person in a bad mood, call center worker, cafeteria staff, your kids)?

Versailles. Looking for
Louis' Throne

Versailles.
Looking for Louis' Throne

f you've never visited Versailles Palace, outside Paris, this story contains several tips, the first of which I'll give you now: if you go, it's a big place; you'll want to wear comfortable shoes.

I'm glad I did, because this story also involves a little bit of running on my part. I had signed up for a 90-minute tour in the Palace. While I waited for the tour to begin, I was wandering around, exploring the gardens, when I realized I only had five minutes before my tour started. So I took off, sprinting down the garden's beautifully manicured wide avenues then across a huge courtyard. When I finally reached the entrance, it occurred to me that I really needed 'to go' (as in, to the ladies' room). The problem was, the public toilets were back across the courtyard I'd just passed and there were at least 30 women waiting in line, not to mention I'd have to pay to use one of those public toilets. None of this was working for me.

So I decided to ask the woman at the reception desk if I could use one of the restrooms in the building where my tour was starting. Now, I knew she was going to say no, so I knew I had nothing to lose – why not ask?

As I approached her desk I consciously stepped into 'Partner mode'. I made eye contact and smiled. "You wouldn't have a bathroom here I could use, would you?" I asked, keeping my energy upbeat while using my very best French. "Public toilets are across the courtyard," came her curt response.

And this is where the magic happened... Even though I was less than pleased with her decision, I smiled, nodded, maintained eye contact and held onto my upbeat energy, "merci, quand même," (thanks anyway)... and just as I turned to leave and walk away, she spoke.

"But we can make an exception for you."

Holy Smoly Canoly, Batman, I thought! How did that happen?!

Then she added, "I'm not really supposed to do this." Using our best Pink Panther impersonation, no-one-sees-us-doing-this, we tiptoed across the busy lobby to the private bathroom for employees.

"I'm sorry it isn't nicer." Wow, now she was apologizing.

I was thinking, *hey, sweetheart, I wasn't expecting Louis' throne! Heck it has a door, no line and I don't have to pay*. I gave her a big smile and a "merci beaucoup"!

Staying Detached from the Outcome

Let me illustrate this technique by sharing another story with you.

Several years earlier on a trip back to Switzerland from California, I had three suitcases and knew full well that airline regulations would not allow me to check all three in without excess baggage fees. I was feeling rather confident (some may call it 'cocky'), assuming that my special communication skills would help me with the check-in agent to avoid having to pay extra fees. I was just starting out in business on my own and had to be a little tight with money. I really didn't want to pay extra charges. That was my downfall; I was attached to the outcome. The whole interaction with the agent was a power struggle; me trying to coerce him 'nicely' into making an exception for me, the agent exercising his discretionary effort (against my favor) and power to say no, just because he could. Much to my dismay, that lesson cost me $100.

What I realized from that experience was that I was attached to the outcome. I wanted what I wanted and tried to force 'my way' with an unsuccessful result. If you have ever attempted to convince a toddler of something they didn't want to do, you know what I'm talking about. The bad news is this approach doesn't generally improve the outcome with a two-year-old. The good news is, more often than one might expect, it will improve the outcome with most people over 4 ft/120 cm. Learning from this experience, I was able to remain detached from what I wanted with the woman in Versailles and as a result, magic happened!

Partner Mindset Technique No. 6

Partner
Mindset
Technique
No. 6

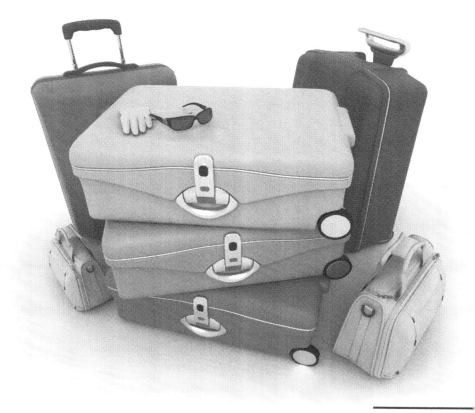

Key Concepts

What is important to know is that people have something called 'discretionary effort'. Discretionary effort, which I referred to in the prior technique, is a concept which my brother, Kevin learned many years ago. Imagine in a work situation: on average, how much effort do people put in to completing a task or their work? For most people, it would be about 70-80% of their capacity. This means they have an additional 20-30% additional effort at their disposal to tap into. Anytime you meet someone, they have at their discretion, the ability to make your life easier or more difficult. Imagine a CEO who passes a janitor in the hallway rushing by without greeting them, business as usual. Now rewind the scenario and as the CEO passes, he or she gives the janitor an upbeat "hello," (using their name gets them bonus points). The janitor responds with a friendly "hello," then

adds, "be careful, the floor is slippery over there." Now the CEO is more likely to spend a pleasant weekend with his or her family instead of at the hospital having a cast put on. When people feel motivated, they are more willing to tap into that discretionary effort that can make your life easier. By using these Partner mindset techniques, you are helping others to increase their motivation to do that!

One explanation why people are motivated to help each other is due to what's called an 'open loop' system, a concept discussed in Daniel Goleman's book, *Primal Leadership*. It means we, as human beings, are hardwired to be affected by each other. Our brain's emotional center, known as the limbic system, is an open loop, which is susceptible to our interactions with others and directly affects how we feel. As a result, someone will be more likely to give you what you want if he or she feels positively motivated to do so. The trick here is to remain in Partner mode even when you don't get what you want. Resist showing your frustration by becoming an aggressive Predator or avoid crumbling into a disappointed Prey. The woman at Versailles let me use the restroom because I continued to treat her with respect, even when she didn't give me what I wanted. Ironically, this made her want to give it to me. So expect seemingly magical outcomes, which will happen with surprising frequency.

Moment of Truth

What is a recent situation when you have been attached to the outcome with a complete stranger (for example, while driving, shopping, in a restaurant, waiting in line at the bank, cinema or airline check-in counter)?

_____

_____

_____

Looking back at that specific situation, how would you behave in a more Partner-like way to give the impression of being detached from the outcome?

_____

_____

_____

What happens when you behave this way? How do you benefit from tapping into others' discretionary efforts?

_____

_____

_____

Green Suede Jacket

Green Suede Jacket

This story highlights the following concepts and Partner mindset techniques:

- **Discretionary effort**
- **Staying detached from the outcome**
- **Being the best customer you can be**
- **Stay upbeat and friendly, even when you don't get what you want**

On a cold and dreary day, just before Christmas 2006, my sister, Pat and I were power walking in a shopping mall in Seattle. The problem is, Pat and I like to shop, so using the mall to exercise was a slightly dangerous proposition. The pre-Christmas sales were in full swing and, just as we were circling the top floor for the second time – there it was, in the window of Coldwater Creek – a green suede jacket. I'm slightly obsessed with a particular shade of green (OK, extremely obsessed) and this jacket was just that color.

"I've got to try it on!" I stopped power walking and just stared at that jacket like some women stare at posters of George Clooney.

We interrupted our power walk and ducked into the store. The jacket fitted me perfectly and was reduced by 25%. Just when I thought, *OK, let's wrap this up and get back to our exercise*, I noticed the collar was wrinkled.

Uh-oh, I thought, *you can't iron suede*. I asked the saleswomen if there was another jacket in the same size, maybe in the back room. She checked. Unfortunately, it was the only one and she suggested I ask the manager for an additional discount.

At the checkout counter, I explained the situation to the manager and showed her the wrinkled collar.

"Would you be willing to give me a further discount? It isn't quite perfect..." I enquired.

"No," she said, "I'm sorry, it's already on sale. I can't discount it any further." As we were standing at the cash register, she asked the next logical question, "Do you still want to buy it?"

The truth is, I was already in love with my new jacket. "Yes, I'll take it anyway, thanks," I said sounding not in the least disappointed. I didn't indicate any annoyance with her, though I knew she had the authority (discretionary effort) to grant me a further discount. Instead, as she scanned the price tag and swiped my credit card, we started chatting. I mentioned that I lived in Switzerland.

"Oh, my friend's daughter lived in Switzerland and just loved it!" she said as she folded my beautiful jacket up with matching green tissue paper. We were off and rolling in a friendly conversation. Then just before she totaled the sale, she said, "you know the jacket is not quite right... I think I can give you a further discount on it."

Pat started kicking me under the counter as if to say, *this stuff we do really works!*

"Oh! That would be great! Thanks!" I said beaming as I got another ten percent off my fabulous green suede jacket, we had a lovely exchange and Pat and I resumed our walk thoroughly pleased with ourselves. I'd even be willing to bet the adrenaline from the added discount helped me burn a few extra calories!

This reaction, I realized, occurs again and again when people really feel like you're genuinely treating them with respect and one of the ways they can tell is that when they don't give you what you want and you're nice to them anyway, they realize, *OK, she's still a nice person and not penalizing me, I can give her what she wants, why not?* This can happen when you stay in Partner and they recognize there are no strings attached.

I have come across two related physiological explanations why this approach is so effective.

The first, explained earlier, is because people are hardwired to want to help each other (remember the 'open loop' system Daniel Goleman talks about). The second explanation is also connected to the brain. Research by Dr Gregory S Berns demonstrated that when we choose a positive response to co-operate with another person instead of an opposing negative response, this behavior activates the joy centers in our brains. We get a hit of pleasure by doing good for others, unofficially known as 'our brain on hugs'.

So, when the manager gave me the discount, she got to feel good about herself for having given me what I wanted!

Moment of Truth

Notice what prevents you from being the best customer you can. What gets in the way for you?

_____

_____

_____

What opportunities do you regularly have to be the best possible customer you can be? (Examples: ask the waiter/waitress's name and use it, if the salesperson looks stressed and you're not in a rush, let them know you have the time and they don't need to hurry, use an upbeat, friendly, relaxed tone when calling tech support, especially if they made the error.)

_____

_____

_____

Now practice being the best customer you can be. Select a specific person/situation. What will you do? How will you behave? What will you say?

_____

_____

_____

Bonus Tip

If you are the best customer you can possibly be, you get even more than you thought possible and life will become easier!

chivalry in the station

Chivalry in the Station

The following is a story where I almost dropped the ball and missed an opportunity to make someone else look good by not accepting their help.

A few years ago, I was getting off a train in Zurich and was wheeling a suitcase behind me down the aisle towards the door. On this rare occasion, I had almost nothing in my suitcase. It was light as a feather!

A gentleman of about 85 was sitting near the door. He said something to me in German. (A little observation about the Swiss culture: it's not uncommon for strangers to look out for others and let them know if they have done, or are about to do, something wrong. Knowing this, you'll understand why I thought, *aaaawww, man, what did I do wrong now?*) I turned around thinking maybe I'd hit someone with my suitcase or run over someone's dog. Not finding anyone in distress, I thought, I don't know what this guy wants from me. So I attempted to block him and said, "Ich spreche kein Deutsch," (I don't speak any German), happy that I had an excuse not to engage further.

Well, another thing to know about the Swiss: they are seriously gifted when it comes to speaking multiple languages. This man heard my accent and said to me in lovely English, "May I help you with your suitcase?" Here I was making up a story that he wanted to tell me I'd done something wrong and all he wanted to do was help me out! (Note to self: remember to apply Partner Technique No. 1: Make up another story – a positive one!) I wasn't going to let an 85 year old man get up to help me with an empty suitcase. Luckily, just before I said *no, thank you*, I caught myself, realizing I was just about to block an offer (a cross-cultural, cross-generational offer at that).

"Oh, that would be lovely," I said, instead.

This man lifted my suitcase from its resting place, took it from the train and standing on the platform, extended his hand to help me off the train. He flashed a proud smile – chivalry at its best! It was like a scene in a movie from the turn of the century. I was half expecting to see vapor from a steam train as I descended the steps. I don't know who left in a better mood – me or the elderly gentleman! I was happy I'd remembered to accept the offer before it was too late and felt the benefits of that simple acceptance for hours afterwards.

Remember the brain research, human beings are hardwired to want to help others. Selfishly, it makes us feel good when we do good deeds for others. When we accept an offer from another person, even when we don't really need it, it's a way of stepping into Partner mode. Accepting the offer is a way of advancing the relationship and making your Partner look (and feel) good!

President Woodrow Wilson

Accept the Offer

This story highlights a fundamental principle of improvisational theater: always accept the offer. I've been told the concept was first introduced by Viola Spolin in her book *Improvisation for the Theater*. In order for a scene to move forward, actors accept others' ideas, suggestions, realities and invitations. The rule is: if you are not accepting, you are 'blocking the offer' which means you are rejecting it and in essence, rejecting the other person. In improvisational theater, blocking an offer is the greatest of sins for actors because it can halt or kill a scene. In relationships, 'blocking the offer' can cause communication breakdowns between people.

In the real world, human beings are social animals. We are programmed to work together and depend on each other to get things done. Yet we human beings tend to do a lot of blocking, causing unnecessary stress, frustration and conflict with others. Some of the reasons we block offers include: we might not realize an offer has been made, we might feel uncomfortable, especially if it comes from a stranger, accepting offers might mean more work. Sometimes it just feels good to say no – like a source of power – it gives a sense of control to say no to someone or something.

Knowing this is such a strong tendency, I regularly practice 'accepting the offer' – whether I'm in public, at work or with my friends. Kat Koppett, author of *Training to Imagine*, says that accepting the offer is the foundation of all relationships.

Partner
Mindset
Technique
No. 7

TESTIMONIAL

... from Alex, finance director with an NGO (non governmental organisation): "After my presentation last spring, one of my direct reports approached me and asked if he could give me some tips for improving my speech. I was thinking, 'are you joking, who is this kid?' Luckily I caught myself just in time and remembered to accept the offer. I replied, 'sure, let's talk next week back in the office.' This was a smart move as the delay allowed me time to put my ego in check.
In turns out the kid had some great points on improving both the content and layout. Now he is the unofficial 'presentations coach' for the entire office!"

Moment of Truth

Do you block offers before they happen? How?
In all situations, or only some? In which situations
and with whom?

Here's your assignment: for the next 48 hours,
practice accepting every offer that comes your
way, from opening a door to assistance/advice
on a project. Follow the rule: accept the offer.
Never block an offer. (OK maybe not everything…)

What kinds of offers did you get? (An offer can
be verbal, conceptual, physical or emotional.)
Examples: someone offered you their seat on a
crowded bus, a smile, someone let you go ahead
of them in line and so on.

Next, practice extending offers enthusiastically for the next few days. How does it feel when others accept your offers?

_____

_____

_____

How does it feel when they block your offers?

_____

_____

_____

What are some of the rewards and benefits to accepting offers in your life?

_____

_____

_____

Fun Works

Training to Imagine: Practical Improvisational Theatre Techniques to Enhance Creativity, Teamwork, Leadership and Learning by Kat Koppett applies improvisational theater methodologies to developing important business skills. Koppett demonstrates to trainers and managers how they can effectively transfer improv training techniques to their day-to-day business environment.

Even though this book is written for trainers, it also appeals to HR personnel, managers and team leaders who are interested in increasing their tool kit, and enhancing the impact, fun and retention levels of their workshops. No previous experience with improvisation or performing is needed. It offers all the necessary background, providing clear and practical instructions with a range of simple and effective exercises. A few years ago, my family used it for a party theme for my brother, Michael's 50th birthday with great success!

Partner
Mindset
Book
Reference

stopped by a cop

Stopped by a Cop

While reading the following story, see which concepts and Partner mindset techniques you can identify.

It was especially tempting to go Predator or even Prey to get out of the situation I'm about to share with you. This is what happened.

A couple of years ago, I was driving down a road in Vevey, Switzerland, where I now live. I passed a police officer, parked perpendicular to me. We were close enough to make eye contact. As I proceeded down the road, a car coming toward me flashed its lights at me. At that moment, I realized that I was driving down a one-way street the wrong way with a cop as my eye witness! *What do I do now,* I thought? I took the first turn I could to at least show the cop, *hey, I'm trying to correct my error.* Most unfortunately, I found myself going down yet another one-way street the wrong way!

At this point, I figured I'd better just park the car because this was only going to get worse and I suspected the cop was close behind. At least it wouldn't look like I was running from anything. So I parked the car and about 30 seconds later the cop showed up with sirens blaring...

This guy looked like something out of a Clint Eastwood movie. He sauntered over to my car with his pants tucked into knee-high polished boots. He spoke aggressively to me in French as if he was scolding a dog.

"Do you know what you did!? Do you know how dangerous that was?" He held his hands on his hips, making himself even broader.

I had been warned about being stopped by the police in Switzerland. I knew it wasn't like getting pulled over in the United States where you can sometimes laugh and talk nicely to the police officer and get off with just a warning, or even a wave of the hand. Not so, I'd heard, in Switzerland. You get pulled over in Switzerland, you get a ticket.

Still, I knew I had a choice in my attitude. In the thirty seconds before the cop showed up I asked myself, given the fact that I knew I was going to get the ticket, *Amy what do you want to have happen in this situation?* I decided I'd prefer it not to be an emotionally painful experience. That was what I was going for. So I said to myself, *Amy, just use your Partner skills and do the best you can.*

When he reached my car and spoke in such a hostile, disrespectful manner I momentarily considered my other fantasy choices. I could respond like a Predator, which would have sounded something like, *yeah, yeah, I know, whatever. Alright, just give me the ticket, will you?* (sounding annoyed and impatient). I figured, he was going to give me the ticket anyway, why let him disrespect me, too?

The alternative response, on the off-chance that it might work, was the semi-pathetic, sobbing Prey reaction: babbling about being a foreigner and female, crying and apologizing for my errors. (OK, so I wasn't proud of this moment of weakness, though it did work particularly well once on a highway in Ohio.)

Instead I resisted both temptations and decided to use the situation to practice staying in Partner mode. I did this by the way I interacted with him.

"Your documents!" he commanded.

I slowly leaned over to get the paperwork out of the glove compartment. I could feel the nervous energy increasing and did everything I could to control my movements, staying slow and steady. I gave him the papers. I looked him in the eyes.

"Oui, monsieur," I responded to some questions, as calmly as I could.

"Non, monsieur," I responded at the appropriate moments, just as calmly.

I offered no defensive reaction, nor explanation. He looked at my driver's license.

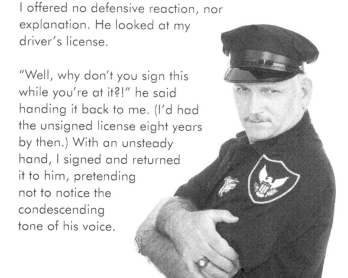

"Well, why don't you sign this while you're at it?!" he said handing it back to me. (I'd had the unsigned license eight years by then.) With an unsteady hand, I signed and returned it to him, pretending not to notice the condescending tone of his voice.

Then he began to circle the car. I knew what he was doing. He was looking for other violations to add: bald tires, wrong tires for the season, whatever he could find. Regularly, Swiss cops pull people over for this check alone and it can be quite costly if they find you in violation of something. The funny part was that I'd had the tires replaced just the day before. I had to fight the temptation to lean out the window and yell, *yeah, you look at those tires! If you look close enough, you'll see the chalk marks still on them*! Amazingly, I maintained my composure.

He returned to my window and seemed a little frustrated not to have found anything wrong. So what did he do? He yelled the same thing at me in the same voice, "do you know what you did!? Do you know how dangerous that was?!"

Haven't we had this conversation? I was tempted to respond. Instead, I again resisted the temptation and answered his questions with a simple, "oui, monsieur. Non, monsieur."

Then he stood there for a moment.

"This would have cost you a lot of money," he said gruffly.

As this whole conversation was in French, I remember the first thing I did was to translate the past tense of 'will' and 'would have'. Then I realized, holy smokes!!! I'm not getting a ticket! He handed me back my paperwork and walked away. I sat in my car for several minutes, too shocked to do anything except wonder how that just happened.

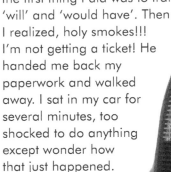

I think what worked in this situation was that I became neither whiny/manipulative nor aggressive/defensive with him. I believe these are the reactions to which police officers are most accustomed. I made a conscious choice to put my ego to the side, I resisted the justifiable temptation to defend myself and when he asked the questions, I communicated respect for both of us. And because I didn't appear to take offense at his aggressiveness, it was as if I didn't give him a good enough reason to issue me a ticket.

What are the concepts and 4 Partner mindset techniques I applied?

Go to my website for the answer CarrollCoaching.com

For me, this is an example of how magic can happen. When you think there is a definite, predictable conclusion – things can change. Even when you're sure of an outcome, magic can happen. When someone is anticipating an aggressive or defensive reaction and instead receives a calm, respectful response, it can be incredibly disarming.

Moment of Truth

Where do you say, "yes, but...!" For example, "yes, but, I have the right to defend myself in this situation!" Where could you give up the right to defend yourself, or even the desire to be right in order to get a different outcome (for example, you miss an important meeting with a colleague and discover that you both marked down different dates in your agendas. He implies you got the date wrong. You know for a fact, he got it wrong. In the meeting he was to share some information with you in order to complete an important project. Instead of insisting he made the mistake, you choose to reply, "I may have confused the dates. Are you available to speak on Wednesday?")

List particular people or situations when it is tempting or even enjoyable to point out how wrong they are:

_____

_____

_____

What could you gain if you give up the need and desire to be right? In the example opposite, the relationship with your colleague is likely to go undamaged, plus it's possible the colleague may also take responsibility for confusing the dates. In addition, by preserving the relationship, you get more of what you want. In the opposite example, the much needed knowledge to get the project completed.

How could you imagine responding in a way where you give up the right to be right?

Another Reason
to Check your Ego

As you can see with these many stories and scenarios, it's clear how much our ego affects our mood, behaviors and actions. This is just the beginning. If you are ready to advance to the next level of personal awareness and empowerment, I highly recommend the following book: *A New Earth* by Eckhart Tolle.

In this book, Tolle shows you the mechanics behind the ego that can lead to a shift in consciousness, that can lead to greater inner peace and happiness. If spirituality is not your thing, don't let that get in the way. This book is extraordinary!

check your

ego

Start Every Relationship as if it is Forever

Luggage Lost in Translation

Last year, my colleague, Robbie and I were flying economy from Russia to Seattle with an overnight stay in London. Somewhere along the way, our suitcases went missing. When we arrived in Seattle, we were seriously jetlagged with no luggage and had to give a workshop. Not a pretty situation. Even worse, this was the third time in a row that Robbie's luggage had been lost with the same airline company! Robbie, normally lives and breathes the Partner mindset. This was the last straw for him. I suspected the heat I could feel nearby was fire coming from his ears.

Luckily, Robbie has a very high level of emotional intelligence, so by the time we found the airline personnel who was going to fill out paperwork to track the lost luggage, Robbie had managed to cool off and drag himself back into Partner mode.

We must have spent 45-60 minutes with this airline employee, whose name we learned was Rita and ended up having a lovely chat with her. We discovered she was originally from Romania, at which point Robbie impressed her with his collection of Romanian words. After the paperwork was finally complete, we asked if there was some compensation for us. She apologized and explained that she could only offer us $75 each since we flew economy. We accepted the compensation enthusiastically, even though I knew it wasn't even going to cover the cost of replacing my makeup! We thanked Rita and said goodbye.

Two days later we got our suitcases and five days after that, after having checked in on line, we were back at the Seattle airport. We stopped by the counter to drop off our luggage when lo and behold, we saw Rita! I mean, seriously, has that ever happened to you that you see the same airline employee twice? And if it has happened to you, you are traveling way too much!

Rita spotted us, gave an enthusiastic wave and motioned us to come over.

"I see you received your suitcases, I'm so glad!" she said. Then her face suddenly turned serious, peering over her glasses. "Please give me your tickets," she instructed. I was about to explain that we had already checked in when Robbie elbowed me to shut up. Rita disappeared into an office and came back moments later with two seats upgraded to business class!

Now, seriously, would that ever have happened if we hadn't been incredibly pleasant with Rita during the dreaded paperwork five days prior? Hmmmm, I guess we will never know for sure... What this has taught me is to start every relationship as if it is forever. The benefit is twofold, first of all, it counts as 'going to the gym'. The more I practice, the better I get. The second reason to start every relationship as if it is forever is because, you never know!

My brother, sister and I keep a running tab of who gets the most perks from using these techniques, concepts and attitude. My brother sent us an email, "I got a free bottle of wine on a flight today because I was friendly with the flight attendant." (We agreed my business class upgrade on a transatlantic flight trumped his bottle of wine.) These techniques pay off in surprising ways. You might want to keep your own list of payoffs. This will help reinforce the power you have to get more of what you want, more often with less hassle.

conclusion:

Introducing the Chicken Dance

Conclusion: Introducing the Chicken Dance

Throughout these stories, you can see the rewards reaped by applying the Partner mindset in a wide variety of situations. Life keeps getting easier. There's less conflict, less resistance. It can also be extremely entertaining and empowering. I have unbelievable power to influence the people and situations around me and so do you. What's more, I benefit from discounts to upgrades to better relationships. Life is rich. I'll leave you with a last story from my personal life, because the rewards may be greatest there.

A friend and I were on the beach in Greece a couple of years ago, when she told me a powerful story. Here's how it went.

There was a woman, Isabelle, who had a tense and difficult relationship with her teenaged stepdaughter who visited her and her husband each summer. This summer in particular, Isabelle was especially nervous because the visit was to be extended. She was anxious about how she would manage the tension and avoid the numerous conflicts of the past.

Isabelle had been doing pretty well managing herself, until about ten days into the visit; things broke down one evening at the dinner table. Her stepdaughter had been there long enough that the initial welcome, novelty and pleasantries had worn off. Tensions were running high. When her stepdaughter made a derogatory comment about the food, Isabelle felt herself losing her cool. She was seeing broccoli au gratin flying across the table, then she suddenly remembered a technique someone had once told her about. It involved doing something completely different and unexpected during moments of stress. So, instead of exploding verbally like Isabelle had done in the past, she calmly put down her fork, stood up, pushed back her chair and proclaimed in a booming Master of Ceremonies voice, "IT IS NOW TIME… FOR THE CHICKEN DANCE!" Isabelle proceeded to fold her hands up under her armpits, flapped her makeshift wings and began squawking loudly, strutting like a chicken on Red Bull across the kitchen floor. The whole family was stunned into silence then a moment later, burst into laughter. After a minute, Isabelle calmly sat back down and said with a smile, "would you pass the broccoli?"

When I heard this story, I immediately sent an e-mail to my boyfriend back in Switzerland. He had let me know before leaving for Greece that my bursts of anger, when directed his way, weren't working for him.

He'd requested that when I get angry, I speak to him more calmly. The problem was, these angry reactions felt so difficult to control; I had no idea what else to do. The Chicken Dance offered me an alternative!

I had the opportunity to practice the technique one night not long after that. We had driven from our home in Vevey to Geneva to attend a Ben Harper concert. Arriving a little late, the parking lot was packed. After driving around for about 20 minutes, we spotted a parking place in the next lane over. I was driving, so I asked my boyfriend to hop out and stand in the spot to save it. I drove the car around the long aisle, only to find him standing in front a car that had just entered our spot!

I looked at him.

"What happened?!" I asked with, perhaps, a bit too much energy.

My boyfriend got back in the car and explained that someone came up and aggressively took the parking spot. I was furious that he would give in and lose our spot so quickly. In that moment, in a low voice he asked me, "honey, is it time for The Chicken Dance?" It clearly was. As soon as I started squawking and flapping my elbows, we were laughing and ended up having a great evening.

The Chicken Dance is a way to shift your mood quickly. It is a powerful technique you can use to alter your behaviors and attitude.

Moment of Truth

And for your last exercise:

When there are events that upset you at work or at home, what are some Chicken Dance strategies you could use in personal and professional settings?

Warning: if you risk losing your job by doing The Chicken Dance at work, it may not be appropriate. An alternative idea to The Chicken Dance strategy is to speak gibberish for one or two minutes with a strange accent. (Think outrageous and positive.)

_____

_____

_____

_____

_____

_____

_____

_____

You can use these skills and concepts across the entire spectrum of your life. When you practice bringing awareness to your reactions by employing the behaviors discussed here, you will change the dynamics and reap the rewards in every area of your life. Use them continuously and you'll get better, faster. Practicing with strangers makes it easier, kind of like having an extra set of wheels when first learning to ride a bicycle. The payoff will be even greater in the relationships that are most important to you.

TESTIMONIAL

The week after an intensive leadership training, David, a manager at a European telecommunications company, wrote this: "Amy, I've started using what you taught us 'in the field', especially with people I used to have issues with. I'm already having excellent results. Thank you so very, very much."

During training and coaching sessions, people often ask: "when is it appropriate to go Predator or Prey?" This is where these techniques become philosophical. I tell them the standard I hold myself to (which I don't always achieve): "the only time either response is justifiable is when my life or someone else's life is at risk." That may sound like an unrealistic standard, which is why I'm not always successful at achieving it in the moment. By holding myself to such a high standard, I'm able to remain in Partner mode more and more often. In fact, my opinion on this philosophy has begun to shift slightly. I was recently hired to give communication training for the United Nations in Geneva. As a part of the extensive hiring process, I was required to take a four hour

on line exam. It covered a multitude of scenarios, including what to do if you are ever taken hostage. My first thought was, *I'm doing communication trainings in Geneva, I don't think this will be an issue.* Then after I reflected a moment I thought, *hmm maybe I can learn something here.* Sure enough, I did. The recommendation from the UN is, if you are a hostage, never cry, plead or beg for your life. So naturally, I analyzed this through the Predator, Prey or Partner™ model. Essentially, they are saying *don't go Prey, even when your life is at risk.* What we do know is that when people are 'too nice, too submissive, too pathetic', it can actually trigger a Predator response in another person. I now believe that if I were ever in a situation that was truly life-threatening, depending on the circumstances, I would do everything I could to control my emotions and continue to maintain a respectful Partner mindset.

Master Your Mood

Daniel Goleman is famous for his work with 'emotional intelligence', and co-authored a book published in 2002 called *Primal Leadership: Realizing the Power of Emotional Intelligence*. I highly recommend it, especially for anyone in a role of leadership, whether in the business world or a social environment. You will discover how the leader's mood has a very direct effect on others' attitudes, results and the bottom line.

Leadership Presence: Dramatic Techniques to Reach Out, Motivate and Inspire

Another useful resource is *Leadership Presence: Dramatic Techniques to Reach Out, Motivate and Inspire*. In it, authors Belle Linda Halpern and Kathy Lubar create a practical guide for translating acting techniques into leadership presence. The authors show you how to apply qualities to connect authentically in order to motivate and inspire the people you lead while achieving business results.

Partner Mindset Reading Suggestions

Keep in mind: I wouldn't want to suggest that applying the philosophy and techniques in these stories will completely eliminate all stress, tension or conflict from your relationships. At the same time, be prepared for magic to happen and discover how you can get more of what you want, more often with less hassle!

A request: please send me your Partner-in-Action mindset stories and successes! I'd be delighted to hear how you've used these techniques and the rewards you've reaped as a result. Send them to me at Amy@CarrollCoaching.com or through my web site: www.CarrollCoaching.com.

Good luck and thanks for reading. Be sure to keep an eye out for advanced lessons and 'dance steps' in *Undoing the Ego Tango: Learning the Fancy Footwork* available soon on DVD.

about the author

Photos by Stefan Heinz

Amy brings with her over 25 years of personal experience and education. Fourteen of those years were spent working in psychiatric, managed care and educational facilities before becoming a coach, trainer and speaker.

Her understanding of the human psyche is extensive.

About the Author

Amy calls upon her education in psychology, improvisational theater, mediation and NLP (neuro linguistic programming) to lead training and coaching programs for multinationals worldwide, working independently and in partnership with SkillsToSuccess Inc, RC Komm S.A. and TNM Coaching.

Amy is a Master Practitioner of NLP, a Professional Certified Coach, member of the International Coach Federation and has completed the coaching curriculum of CoachU, the foremost coaching institution in the world. She coaches clients to become more dynamic, powerful and persuasive communicators, developing their ability to influence others by creating powerful partnerships. She does this with the help of the improvisational theatre philosophy, 'make your partner look good!'

Being one of the youngest of seven children taught Amy a lot about communicating for impact! She has coached whole families, MBA students, high-ranking executives and nonprofit leaders around the world. Her extensive client list includes blue chip multinational software and IT companies, world-wide manufacturers of household name brands, international shipping and communications companies and leading humanitarian organisations.

References

Debbie Ford, 1999, *The Dark Side of the Light Chasers: Reclaiming Your Power, Creativity, Brilliance and Dreams*, New York (NY, USA), Riverhead Trade. http://www.debbieford.com

Stephen Covey, 2004, *The 7 Habits of Highly Effective People,* Bath (UK), Simon & Schuster Ltd. http://www.stephencovey.com

Marshall B. Rosenberg, 2003, *Nonviolent Communication: A Language of Life*, Encinitas (CA, USA), PuddleDancer Press. http://www.cnvc.org/en/about/marshall-rosenberg.html

George Kohlrieser, 2006, *Hostage at the Table: How Leaders Can Overcome Conflict, Influence Others, and Raise Performance*, San Francisco (CA, USA), Jossey-Bass. http://www.hostageatthetable.com

Daniel Goleman, 2006, *Emotional Intelligence: Why it Can Matter More Than IQ,* New York (NY, USA), Bantam Dell. http://www.danielgoleman.info/blog

Daniel Goleman, Richard Boyatzis and Annie Mckee, 2002, *Primal Leadership; Realizing the Power of Emotional Intelligence*, Boston (MA, USA), Harvard Business School Publishing. http://www.danielgoleman.info

Viola Spolin, 1999, *Improvisation for the Theater: A Handbook of Teaching and Directing Techniques,* Northwestern University Press, Reed Business Information, Inc. http://www.spolin.com

Kat Koppett, 2001, *Training to Imagine: Practical Improvisational Theatre Techniques to Enhance Creativity, Teamwork, Leadership and Learning,* Virginia (USA), Stylus Publishing. http://www.koppett.com

Eckhart Tolle, 2006, *A New Earth: Awakening to Your Life's Purpose,* USA, The Penguin Group. http://www.eckharttolle.com

Belle Linda Halpern and Kathy Lubar, 2003, *Leadership Presence: Dramatic Techniques to Reach Out, Motivate and Inspire*, New York (NY, USA), Gotham Books.

References

Mastering the
Art and Science
of Positive Influence

Carroll Communication Coaching
Rue de l'Union 20
1800 Vevey
Switzerland

+ 41 21 534 7214
+ 41 79 653 5423

amy@carrollcoaching.com

www.carrollcoaching.com

11641302R00076

Made in the USA
Charleston, SC
11 March 2012